RECENT REVOLUTIONS
IN PHYSICS

RECENT REVOLUTIONS
IN PHYSICS
the subatomic world

BY ALBERT STWERTKA

FRANKLIN WATTS 1985
NEW YORK LONDON
TORONTO SYDNEY
A SCIENCE IMPACT BOOK

Diagrams by Vantage Art, Inc.

Photographs courtesy of:
Stanford Linear Accelerator Center: pp. 24, 27;
Fermilab, Chicago: p. 28;
Brookhaven National Laboratory: pp. 33, 50.

Library of Congress Cataloging in Publication Data

Stwertka, Albert.
Recent revolutions in physics.

(A Science impact book)
Includes index.
Summary: Looks at recent developments in the field
of elementary particle physics, discussing matter,
relativity, atom composition, the nuclear atom, quarks,
and gravitational and electromagnetic force.
1. Particles (Nuclear physics)—Juvenile literature.
[1. Particles (Nuclear physics) 2. Nuclear physics]
I. Title.   II. Series.
QC793.27.S78 1985   539.7'21   85-7623
ISBN 0-531-10066-9

CONTENTS

RECENT REVOLUTIONS
IN PHYSICS

CHAPTER 1
THE RAW MATERIAL OF MATTER

*W*hat is matter made of? Scientists and philosophers have been trying to answer this question for more than two thousand years. Only recently have they taken great strides in discovering the forces that govern all matter in the universe. Their search into the subatomic world was helped by startling new ideas and amazing new tools. The so-called atom smashers of fifty years ago have evolved from laboratory gadgets to giant, mile-long, high-energy machines that act as nuclear probes. Future designs now being considered at research facilities will reach some one hundred miles (161 km) in circumference at a cost that only national governments can afford.

One of the primary goals of physics—to find a unified theory of all the forces in the universe—has almost been reached. For many of the world's physicists, the vast riddle of the structure of matter is nearing a solution. The new discoveries made in the field of high-energy physics have profoundly affected our views of the physical universe and how it began.

Since the beginning of the twentieth century, physicists have examined matter at smaller and smaller distances. As the machines for probing matter became larger and more energetic, successive layers, or substructures, of matter were discovered and investigated. Almost like peeling the skin off an onion, scientists removed one layer of matter to reveal the next one. There are very strong reasons to believe that the ultimate constituents of matter have finally been reached. The new elementary particles, the "stuff" out of which everything else is made, appear to be divided into two classes: the leptons and the quarks.

To understand the significance of quarks and leptons, and to appreciate the profound changes that have taken place in the world of science, we must first start with a look at the atom. The remarkable series of experimental and theoretical successes that led to the discovery of these strange-sounding bits of matter started with the realization that atoms are not fundamental, but composed of other particles.

ELEMENTARY BUILDING BLOCKS

As you know, the objects of our everyday life—the food we eat, the clothes we wear, the air we breathe—are all made up of *atoms*. Only ninety-two different kinds of atoms are found in nature. This small number of components forms the infinite variety of natural materials that make up our world.

The concept of a set of elementary building blocks from which complex systems are made is very appealing. The idea was first proposed by the Greek philosophers as far back as the fourth and fifth centuries B.C. The very name for these building blocks comes from the Greek word *atomos*, which means indivisible.

It was not until late in the nineteenth century, however, that the existence of atoms was firmly established. Atoms were first thought of as small, hard spheres without any internal parts. But scientists soon came to understand that there were many different kinds of atoms, making up the different elements. As the properties of the various atoms became better understood, similarities between different elements led to the discovery that atoms could be placed into families with similar chemical behavior. But why did different atoms have similar properties? The regularity with which these properties repeated themselves hinted at a more complex structure of the atom.

ATOMIC STRUCTURE

The discovery of the *electron* by J. J. Thomson in 1897 and the realization that all atoms contain electrons provided the first important insight into the composition of the atom.

Electrons are negatively charged particles, thousands of times lighter in weight, or mass, than the atoms that contain them. Since it was known that under ordinary conditions atoms are electrically neutral, scientists knew that the negative charge of the electrons must be balanced by some positive charge. In 1912 Thomson identified the positively charged component of the atom. Using the same techniques he had employed for electrons, he discovered the *proton*, a particle with a mass 1,836 times that of the electron, and a positive electrical charge.

Thus it was established that every electron in the atom was complemented by a proton. But when techniques for careful measurements were developed, it became obvious that in most atoms the combined mass of electrons and protons still did not account for the atom's entire mass. There had to be another, yet undiscovered component.

The mystery of the missing mass was finally cleared up in 1932 by the English physicist James Chadwick. He discovered an electrically neutral particle within the atom which he called a *neutron*. He measured the mass of the neutron and found it to be slightly greater than the mass of a proton.

These three atomic particles—electrons, protons, and neutrons—came to be thought of as the fundamental components of all atoms. The atoms of different elements were simply made up of different numbers of protons, neutrons, and electrons.

THE NUCLEAR ATOM

Now that the atom was known to have internal parts, researchers confronted the puzzle of how the fundamental particles all fit together. For a time, the atom was thought of as a sphere of positively charged matter in which the electrons were embedded like raisins in a cake. This came to be called the "plum pudding" model of the atom.

One way to find out what is inside a plum pudding is to put your thumb in it. Ernest Rutherford, one of the great innovators of English physics, led a group that developed a technique for doing this. In the process of studying radioactivity, he and his students developed a probe that used positively charged particles, called alpha particles, emitted by certain radioactive uranium salts. They directed a beam of alpha particles toward a very thin gold foil and observed how the particles scattered. Rather than probing with a thumb, this team of physicists fired atomic bullets at the plum pudding.

This method of exploration has been likened to shooting bullets through a large box that contains only a small piece of lead. Most of the bullets would pass right through and out the other side. Occasionally, however, a bullet would hit the lead and ricochet off at some angle. If large numbers of bullets were fired, so that the hidden piece of lead was hit often enough to produce ricochets in various directions, it might be possible to identify the size and shape of the hidden piece of lead.

Rutherford found that most of the alpha particles penetrated the gold foil rather easily. A few, however, were scattered at rather large angles. Some even bounced back. Rutherford was amazed. He wrote, "It was as incredible as if you fired a 15-inch shell at a piece of tissue paper and it came back and hit you." He interpreted these results to mean that while most of the atom is empty space, there is a small, massive, positively charged nucleus at its center, capable of deflecting alpha particles through large angles. Triumphantly Rutherford reported, "Now I know what the atom looks like!" The pudding model was wrong. Instead, the concept of the nuclear atom was born.

The results of this so-called scattering experiment led to a model of the structure of the atom that resembles our solar system. In this model all of the positive charge of the atom is concentrated in a tiny nucleus at its center. The negatively charged electrons surround the nucleus, and rotate in various orbits, just as the planets rotate about the sun. In place of gravity, this miniature "solar" system is held together by the force of attraction between positive and negative charges.

THE STRONG FORCE

But what holds the nucleus together? After all, the only charged particles contained in the nucleus are positively charged. But positive charges repel each other. It is known that the closer together the charges, the greater the force of repulsion.

Rutherford was able to estimate the size of the nucleus, and found it to have a radius some 100,000 times smaller than that of the atom—as small, comparatively, as a speck of dust in a large classroom. Yet the nucleus manages to contain all the positively charged protons squeezed together in an incredibly small volume at the center of the atom. By all rights it should blow itself apart.

Most of the nuclei of atoms found in nature are stable. The fact that positively charged protons, along with neutrons, can exist bound together in the dense and small center of the atom must mean that there is yet another interaction present. This other force must be one of attraction, and somehow must balance the electrical repulsion between the protons. This attractive force binding the nucleus together, first called the nuclear force, is now known as the *strong* or *hadronic force*.

The study of the strong force has been a major concern of modern physics. Experiments show that the strong force has a very small range. Unlike the interaction through the force of gravity, for example, which can extend through the vast distances of interstellar space, the strong force acts only within limited distances. The two protons have to be almost touching in order to "feel" the strong force. Once a particle is outside the nucleus, the strong force ceases to exist.

Interestingly enough, the strong force is independent of the electric charge of the interacting particles. Thus the strong interaction between protons is exactly the same as the strong interaction between a proton and neutron, or between neutrons. Inside a nucleus, therefore, protons and neutrons appear to have similar properties. This equivalence has led to the use of the term *nucleon* to describe both the proton and the neutron. A nucleus such as that of uranium 235, for example, which contains 143 neutrons and 92 protons, is said to contain 235 nucleons. Other properties of this strong nuclear force will be discussed in chapters to follow.

THE NEUTRINO

The hope that all matter might be a combination of electrons, protons, and neutrons was short-lived. As physicists probed the nucleus with more and more powerful machines, and as they studied the phenomenon of radioactivity, new particles appeared.

Radioactivity is associated with the emission of radiation by certain elements such as radium and uranium. These elements have nuclei that are unstable and spontaneously transform themselves into new elements. Energy is given off in the process, in the form of radiation. The kind of radiation emitted depends on the particular species of radioactive atom undergoing the transformation.

Certain radioactive materials give off radiation in the form of electrons—the process is called beta decay. (The electron was called a "beta" particle early in its history, before it was more precisely identified.) Scientists could calculate exactly how much energy should be released in such a radioactive transformation. They soon noticed, however, that some of the emitted electrons had less energy than calculations had predicted. Where was the missing energy? Rather than abandon the strongly held belief that energy can never disappear, they were forced to guess at the existence of a new, experimentally unobserved particle. They named it the *neutrino* ("little neutral one"). They concluded that the neutrino must be carrying off the missing energy.

Until then, neutrinos had always escaped detection. No laboratory detector was sensitive enough to note their presence. They carry no electric charge and can penetrate matter easily because they are immune to both the electromagnetic and the strong force. Because of this almost total lack of interaction, ordinary matter is nearly transparent to neutrinos. Out of ten billion neutrinos passing through an object as large as the earth, for example, only one is likely to interact.

The existence of this extremely elusive particle was finally conclusively established in 1956 by the American physicists Frederick Reines and Clyde L. Cowan, Jr. Working in an underground room of a large nuclear reactor at Savannah

River, they finally saw reactions that could only be explained by the existence of the neutrino. A nuclear reactor was required for this brilliant experiment, because a reactor is an excellent source of large numbers of neutrinos.

Neutrinos are often described as ghost particles. Recording their fleeting presence usually requires detectors of monumental proportions. A "neutrino telescope," for example, is currently being built near Hawaii. It will be used to detect neutrinos generated by energy-producing nuclear processes occurring in the sun and in neighboring galaxies. More than half a billion gallons of water will be kept under observation. An array of cables, each 1,500 feet (457 m) long and carrying light detectors, will be anchored to the floor of the ocean in an attempt to record the faint light produced by the passage of high-energy particles. The array will cover an area that is 750 feet by 750 feet (229 × 229 m).

THE WEAK FORCE

The study of radioactivity led to the discovery of yet another fundamental force (or interaction), the so-called *weak force*. It is the weak force that explains how a nucleus of radium, for example, can transform itself into a different element as it undergoes a radioactive process.

We have seen that in the form of radioactivity known as beta decay, certain radioactive materials spontaneously radiate energy in the form of electrons and neutrinos. The particles emitted by radioactive atoms are known to come from the nucleus. But it is also known that electrons and neutrinos do not exist in nuclei. Where were the electrons coming from? After all, if one sees a person leaving a house, one has to assume that the person was in the house to start with.

The puzzle was solved by the Italian physicist Enrico Fermi, who postulated that the electron and neutrino were first created in some mysterious fashion, and then immediately ejected. His reasoning was based on an analogy with the way ordinary atoms give off energy when they are excited. Sodium vapor lamps, for example, when heated, will begin to glow and emit energy in the form of yellow light. The atoms of sodium tend to rid themselves of excess energy, to "de-excite" themselves, by creating and immediately giving off yellow light.

In a similar manner, the nuclear transformation in beta decay results in a radioactive atom "de-exciting" itself, and going to a more stable form by giving off energy in the form of particles. The force that governs or mediates this transition and results in the creation of two particles, an electron and a neutrino, is called the weak force.

Although the weak force is the least familiar of all the interactions, it nevertheless plays an important role in our ability to live on the earth. We shall see later that the weak interaction provides the first step in the fusion of two protons to form energy in the sun. We shall also see that the weak force was associated with a set of new particles, with the improbable name of *heavy bosons*. The remarkable success in experimentally verifying the existence of the postulated W (W for weak) and Z bosons is a major triumph of modern physics.

VIRTUAL PARTICLES

As particles and forces began to proliferate, scientists focused more closely on the mechanism of their interactions. How does one object actually exert a force on another? The answer to this seemingly innocent question has bothered scientists almost from the moment that the notion of gravity was introduced by Isaac Newton in the eighteenth century. The sun and the earth are some 93 million miles (150 million km) apart, separated by a vacuum, and yet the sun is said to exert a gravitational pull on the earth and keep the earth in orbit.

The problem of how forces make themselves known is not limited to the gravitational interaction. A negatively charged electron that attracts a positively charged proton, even though the charges are separated by a vacuum, is displaying equally puzzling behavior. Electromagnetic forces also act at a distance.

The modern conception of the way particles interact is that they communicate with each other by means of a messenger. Forces are transmitted between particles by the actual exchange of a third particle, called a *virtual particle*. The action of these forces through the exchange of virtual particles can be compared to that of two players throwing a baseball back and forth, where the ball is attached to each player by a spring. Each player exerts a force on the ball, and the effect is as if each exerted a force on the other. A binding force is thereby created between them.

The ghostlike exchange particle, seemingly created out of nothing, is called a virtual particle to distinguish it from a real particle. Under ordinary circumstances it cannot be observed, since its existence would appear to violate the law of conservation of energy. We shall see in a later chapter how quantum mechanics can explain this apparent disregard of one of the most important laws of science. Each of the four fundamental forces—gravitational, electromagnetic, strong, and weak—has a different exchange particle associated with it.

FOUR POWERFUL FORCES

The four basic interactions of matter all differ in their relative strength. Gravity, the force that holds us firmly anchored to the earth, is by far the weakest. Electrical forces are enormous in comparison. The strong force is still more powerful, being approximately one hundred times stronger than even the electromagnetic force, and some ten trillion times stronger than the weak force. Compared with the strong force, the weak force is feeble indeed.

The strength of the interaction is important because it determines the time required for the exchange of its virtual particle. Strong interactions normally take place in about 10^{-23} seconds. This is an incredibly small interval of time. It is equal to approximately the amount of time it would take a beam of light, traveling at 186,000 miles (300,000 km) per second, to pass through an object as small as an atomic nucleus.

We shall see that the strong force is regarded as being strong precisely because it can bring about a change in such a brief interval.

THE REACH OF FORCES

It is striking that the gravitational interaction seems to have no limits in its ability to attract matter over huge distances. For example, galaxies attract other galaxies billions of miles away. Neutrons, on the other hand, must almost be touching before they interact. We intuitively feel, what in effect is true, that the farther away the virtual particle associated with a given force can communicate, the lighter and more mobile it must be.

The range of the force, a measure of how far its influence can be felt, is determined by the mass of its virtual particle. The greater the mass the smaller the range.

Gravitational and electromagnetic forces have essentially infinite ranges and their virtual particles prove to have zero mass. The strong force, on the other hand, has a short range. Its effects hardly extend beyond the nucleus itself. Therefore, its associated virtual particle must have a rather substantial mass. The range of the weak force is even shorter, at most a hundredth that of the strong force. So the weak force must have an even more massive virtual particle. These virtual particles will be discussed more fully in later chapters.

CHAPTER 2
RELATIVITY
AND
UNCERTAINTY

*U*nraveling the microcosm of the atom was made possible by two revolutionary ideas, the special theory of relativity and quantum mechanics. Both of these monumental theories broke in a radical way with previously held concepts of our physical universe.

Einstein's theory of relativity, published in 1905, completely changed our ideas of space and time. It demonstrated the possibility of creating matter. The relationship between energy and matter, now so commonplace, was once considered outlandish. A whole range of phenomena associated with high-energy physics, from the workings of accelerators to the birth and death of particles, would be impossible to comprehend without the theory of relativity.

Quantum mechanics was developed by such celebrated scientists as Louis de Broglie, Max Planck, Werner Heisenberg, and Niels Bohr—names we shall encounter again. Its essential idea was that matter has a dual character. Sometimes it behaved like waves, and sometimes like particles. That matter should have wave properties seemed to violate common sense.

As the theory developed, it also called into question the most basic notions of cause and effect. It was no longer possible to predict precisely the outcome of any experiment. One could only estimate the probability of any particular result. The intuitive feeling of "causality"—something causing something else to happen—was overthrown.

When Einstein said, "God doesn't play dice with the universe," he expressed the reluctance of many scientists to give up the certainties of cause and effect. Give it up they must, however, as quantum physics became one of the most successful theories in the history of physics. Niels Bohr, a strong advocate of the new physics of the quantum, echoed a new generation of physicists when he answered Einstein's famous remark with the words, "Who is Einstein to tell God what to do."

The concepts of the quantum and the creation of matter, as we shall see, play an essential role in understanding what an atom is made of. Modern physics would be unthinkable without these two ideas.

PHOTONS AND ELECTROMAGNETIC ENERGY

Closely related to the growing knowledge of atomic structure was the development of new concepts of radiant, or electro-magnetic, energy. The discovery of the quantum principle by Max Planck in 1900 led the way. It brought the first convincing evidence of the discontinuity of energy. The way light is given off by a red-hot piece of steel, for example, can only be explained by assuming that the radiation is given off discontinuously, in little packages of energy. He named each portion of energy a *quantum,* from the Latin word for "how much."

Planck also found a simple relationship that gave the energy of each package. The rule he formulated states that

$$E = hf$$

To find the energy of a quantum, one multiplies the frequency of the light by a fixed number, a constant, *h,* called Planck's constant. This simple rule forms one of the basic ideas of quantum theory.

Was light a wave or was it a particle? No one who has seen the interference pattern formed by two sources of light—patterns that behave exactly like water waves on a pond—can doubt that light is a wave. But light also behaves like a particle.

The particle properties of light were probably most dramatically illustrated by Einstein's explanation, in 1905, of the so-called photoelectric effect. Einstein, too, postulated that light consists of packages of energy, but visualized them as real particles which he called *photons.* Using Planck's rule to calculate the energy of these photons, he successfully used the concept of the photon to explain the energies observed for electrons emitted from metal surfaces when irradiated by light.

Classical theory had visualized light as a continuous wave of electromagnetic energy spreading out uniformly through space. Einstein's photons, though, introduced a completely novel view. Light could now be considered in an alternative manner, as little grains of energy radiating in a straight line from their source.

It is interesting to note that Einstein was awarded the Nobel Prize for this discovery and not, as is often assumed, for his theory of relativity. Ironically, the photon theory opened the way for the future development of quantum theory, a theory Einstein fought against all his life.

Scientists have had to live with this dual nature of light ever since. Like matter, electromagnetic energy has both wave and particle properties.

SPECIAL THEORY OF RELATIVITY

It was by the theory of relativity that Einstein first demonstrated that energy and matter are completely interchangeable: matter can be created from energy, and energy from matter. Thus the relativity theory is crucial to an understanding of the structure of matter. We shall see that the destruction and creation of particles are essential phenomena that occur frequently in the subatomic world.

Einstein published his famous paper on the special theory of relativity in 1905, the same year as his work on the photoelectric effect. In addition to changing our ideas about time and space, this great work also first demonstrated the relationship between energy and mass with the famous equation

$$E = mc^2$$

where E is the energy equivalent of a given mass m, and c is the velocity of light. The equivalence of mass and energy, which is expressed by the above equation, has become so commonplace today that nuclear physicists usually refer to the mass of a particle in terms of its energy equivalent.

QUANTUM MECHANICS

The central idea associated with quantum mechanics was first put forward by the French physicist Louis de Broglie in 1923. The theory assumed that every material object has a wave property associated with it. Like the photon, matter has a dual nature: it behaves both like a particle and a wave. As soon as wave theory was verified experimentally, it became the long-hoped-for "window" by means of which scientists could look into the atom. Further development by the German physicists Werner Heisenberg and Erwin Schrödinger elevated quantum mechanics to its dominant role in modern physics.

The electron orbiting the nucleus in the simple hydrogen atom, for example, is no longer thought of as a planetary particle. In quantum terms it is conceived as a standing wave extending in a circle around the nucleus. The electron has a wavelength in the same way that a wave on a vibrating string has a wavelength.

As uncomfortable as many physicists feel with the ideas of quantum mechanics (chief among the protesters was Einstein), it has proved itself to be one of the most powerful theoretical conceptions.

HEISENBERG
UNCERTAINTY PRINCIPLE

A profound consequence of representing matter by waves was the limitation it placed on the precision of certain measurements. Until the birth of quantum theory, physicists had assumed that if they knew the position and velocity of a system of particles at any one time, they could predict exactly what those particles would be doing at some future time.

In 1927, however, Werner Heisenberg formulated his famous *uncertainty principle.* It had a profound influence on the development of particle physics. Heisenberg not only demonstrated that we cannot predict the future with absolute certainty, but further showed that we cannot even determine the exact position and velocity of the particles at the present time. Our inability to do so is due to the wave behavior of matter.

Any experiment that tries to measure the energy of a system at a given time will also be affected by the wave nature of matter. The uncertainty principle states that energy and time cannot both be measured simultaneously with unlimited precision.

You can think of it this way: To determine the energy precisely requires a long period of observation. But the longer the time required by the experiment, the less certain we are of when the system had that energy. The more precisely we know the time the measurement was made, the greater the uncertainty in the energy.

THE RANGE OF VIRTUAL PARTICLES

If you now examine the exchange of a virtual particle, it becomes clear why the range is related to its mass. If the virtual particle, or field quantum, as it is sometimes called, has a large mass, its creation, as predicted by the special theory of relativity, must be at the expense of a large quantity of "borrowed" energy. But borrowed from where? The creation of a virtual particle appears to be the making of something out of nothing—a clear violation of the law of conservation of energy. The Heisenberg uncertainty principle, however, tells us that we can violate the conservation of energy as long as the uncertainty in energy exists for a small enough time. We can get away with the violation, that is, as long as no one finds out about it.

The important idea here is that it takes a measurement to detect the violation, and measurements always involve the passage of time. The uncertainty we are permitted is determined by the time interval we use in the measurement. The greater the uncertainty in the energy, the shorter the time the particle can exist: the more energy we borrow, the faster it has to be paid back.

A virtual particle, then, has a life limited by its mass, or energy equivalent. The greater its mass, the greater the energy uncertainty, and the shorter the time for its existence. A short lifetime implies that the distance the particle can travel in any exchange process is limited. A massive virtual particle will therefore have a short range, while a particle like a photon, with zero mass, will have almost an infinite range.

A particle like a proton, then, can be thought of as constantly emitting and reabsorbing virtual particles. The process resembles a juggler tossing balls into the air and catching them again. The only requirement in the quantum world, though, is that the time in the air is short enough to satisfy the uncertainty principle. If some other particle, such as a neutron, now comes close enough to the proton, the neutron can exchange virtual particles with the proton during the brief time the particles are permitted to exist.

THE NONEMPTY VACUUM

Thinking of a vacuum doesn't present much of a problem for most of us. A vacuum is simply a void, a region of space that is completely empty. Nothing exists there, no matter and no energy.

To a physicist, however, a vacuum is a much more complex system. Because of the uncertainty principle there is always the chance that the vacuum can contain a certain amount of energy for a short period of time. The shorter the time, the more energy it can have without our being aware of it. This energy can show itself in many ways. Particles can suddenly be created, and then immediately disappear. Fields can suddenly appear or disappear. This restless vacuum is far from empty; it is swarming with virtual particle pairs, virtual photons, and fields.

FEYNMAN GRAPHS

A very useful method of describing and visualizing some of the exchange interactions discussed was devised by the American physicist Richard P. Feynman. The Feynman graph, as it is called, provides an easily understood picture of a particle event by depicting its evolution—the event before and after its occurrence. In this pictorial representation, time runs along one axis of the diagram, usually from bottom to top, and distance runs along the other axis. To distinguish among various kinds of particles, real particles are represented by straight lines, virtual photons by wavy lines, and virtual particles by dashed lines.

An example using the electromagnetic interaction is shown below in figure 1. Here two electrons approach each other and are scattered after the exchange of a virtual photon.

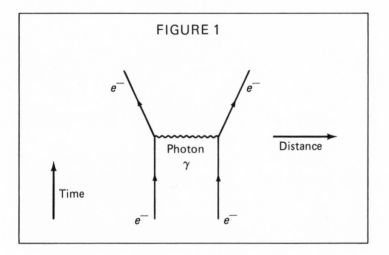

FIGURE 1

CHAPTER 3
GIANT ATOM SMASHERS

A basic paradox of modern high-energy physics is that the smaller the object we want to look at, the larger the observing instrument must be. To be able to "look" into the atom, the world of the inconceivably small, requires monster accelerators that spread across miles of countryside. These giant machines, used to accelerate particles and smash them together, are essential for creating and discovering hitherto unknown particles.

To quote the Italian physicist Carlo Rubbia, co-winner of the 1984 Nobel Prize, "For the man on the street, a collision means destruction. You smash two cars together and you destroy the cars. In particle physics, when you smash two cars together you get twenty new cars."

Working at Harvard and at the Center for European Nuclear Research (CERN) in Geneva, Rubbia has become the model of the modern high-energy physicist who spends as much time in international travel as at the monster accelerators he helps design. To discover new particles, as Carlo Rubbia did in 1974, requires huge accelerators and expenditures of money running into the millions and even billions of dollars. To a certain extent, science today is Big Science. A single experiment can involve hundreds of scientists and technicians. Not only are many universities required to pool their resources, but often international cooperation is necessary.

To produce Professor Rubbia's "new cars," or new particles, requires staggering amounts of energy. What do these accelerators do? Why are they necessary for studying the atom?

ORDERS OF MAGNITUDE

Accelerators produce beams of particles that are made to travel at high speeds—almost at the speed of light—and to collide with certain targets. We need these fast-moving projectiles to penetrate the mighty fields of force that surround the heart of the atom. It is by necessity a "brute force" approach, rather like trying to find out what is inside a package by shooting bullets at it. Observing whether the bullets bounce off at sharp angles, or if strange new pieces emerge from the box, will give us clues to help solve the mystery of the contents of the box.

The particles that are most often used as projectiles are electrons and protons. Electrons appear to lack any further internal structure, which makes them ideal "bullets." They do have a disadvantage, however, in that they radiate away much of their energy as they are accelerated to high speeds. Protons, on the other hand, are much less likely to lose energy but have a more complex structure, being composed of three other particles, the so-called quarks (quarks will be discussed in chapter 6). Because of this complexity, their collisions with atoms can be very complicated, and the process is often compared to smashing Swiss watches together.

The energy of a beam particle is expressed in electron volts, eV. An electron volt is the amount of energy that an electron has when it is accelerated through 1 volt. This is a convenient energy unit because particles of any given energy are so often produced by acceleration through a given voltage. Let's look at an analogy from the world of gravity. An object falling from the top of a building gains energy on the way down. The higher the building, the more energy it will have when it reaches the ground. In the world of electrical fields, the amount of voltage is very similar to height. The more voltage, the more energy. A particle "falling" through 40,000 volts will thus have an energy of 40,000 eV—40,000 times as much energy as the particle falling through 1 volt.

We are accustomed to dealing with relatively low voltages in our everyday life. The familiar "line voltage" in our homes and schools is about 110 volts. The voltage required for a typical television picture tube is about 20,000 volts. Accelerators, though, produce beams with energies ranging from several million volts (MeV) to several billion volts (GeV). These voltages are in the thunderbolt range.

Anyone who has ever worked with high voltage knows how difficult it is to deal with. Not only is it extremely dangerous, but sparking caused by the breakdown of the air or the insulator used to isolate the system makes it almost impossible to sustain the high voltage for any length of time. Many technical and theoretical innovations were needed to attain the voltages achieved by the giant accelerators of today.

SMASHING THE ATOM

The early history of accelerator development, during the 1920s, was very exciting. Scientists throughout the world competed with each other to develop new and more powerful machines. The challenge of probing the atom was taken up by a whole generation of physicists. Who would be the first to develop a machine to smash the atom?

Soon after the end of World War I, Ernest Rutherford had used natural radioactive materials to penetrate the nucleus of a nitrogen atom. Lord Rutherford, who is often called "the father of nuclear physics," successfully accomplished what the medieval alchemists had dreamed of. He "transmuted," or changed, one element into another. He didn't manage to make gold from a base metal, but he did succeed in converting the element nitrogen into oxygen by bombarding the nitrogen with a beam of particles given off by radium. In this technique the projectiles used were relatively low-energy particles emitted by radioactive materials. Their ability to penetrate nuclei was limited to small atoms. New methods were needed that would artificially produce fast, high-energy projectile beams.

Strange machines of all kinds were fabricated. Many laboratories looked like the stage set of a Frankenstein movie, with sparks jumping between large domes and spiral columns. One intrepid scientist even lost his life trying to harness lightning in the Alps. The race was finally won by J. D. Cockraft and E. T. S. Walton at the Cavendish Laboratory in Cambridge. In 1929 they developed a voltage multiplier device that accelerated protons by giving them a huge electrostatic "push" of about 500,000 volts. The speeds attained by the protons were high enough to shatter a lithium atom into its component parts. In 1932, using the voltage multiplier device, they smashed an atom for the first time.

THE CYCLOTRON

One of the losers in the race, however, had an idea that proved to be of even greater importance for the future development of high-energy physics. Ernest O. Lawrence, working at the University of California, had designed a completely different kind of machine, the cyclotron, which did not depend on brute force. Instead of accelerating the particle by giving it one big push, the cyclotron accelerated the particle by a series of many small pushes. The particle, which was made to move in a circle by a magnetic field, was given these pushes on successive turns around the machine. The effect is similar to that of pushing a child on a swing. If each successive push is timed just right, even a series of faint pushes can cause the child to swing in a large arc.

It was no longer necessary to "bust an atom" by producing huge accelerating voltages, usually millions of volts, and applying the full voltage directly across a pair of electrodes. The cyclotron could do the same job with relatively low voltage. Because of this, the cyclotron became the prototype for a succession of cyclic machines that have revolutionized physics. Lawrence's 4-inch (10 cm) tabletop accelerator of the 1930s has developed into machines measured in miles. The early 1-MeV cyclotron became the model for the 30-GeV alternating gradient synchrocyclotron at the Brookhaven National Laboratory, as well as the 400-GeV synchrotrons at the Fermilab, and the Center for European Nuclear Research (CERN) in Geneva.

LINEAR ACCELERATORS (LINACS)

Cyclotrons cost a lot of money. The greater the energy they are designed to supply, the greater the cost. Unfortunately, when electrons are made to move in a circle, they constantly lose energy through a process called synchrotron radiation. The energy is radiated in the form of short-wavelength light. Physicists have estimated the cost of counteracting this loss to increase almost as the cube of the energy. To go from a 100 MeV machine to a 1-GeV machine means that the cost will increase by almost a factor of 1,000.

The linear accelerator was developed to limit the loss of energy through this synchrotron radiation. The particle to be accelerated is made to travel down a series of cylindrical tubes arranged in a straight line. As the particle passes between these "drift" tubes, it is given a series of accelerating pushes by a voltage generator.

The art of constructing linear accelerators has culminated in the two-mile (3 km) long electron linac at Stanford University. It produces electrons of more than 20-GeV energy. A proton linac, constructed in 1972 at the Los Alamos Meson Physics Facility (LAMPF) laboratory in New Mexico, is capable of producing protons with 800-MeV energy.

COLLIDING BEAMS

Until 1965 all accelerators involved in high-energy physics bombarded a stationary target with their fast-moving projectiles. The trouble with a beam of particles hitting a stationary target is that not all the available energy goes into the collision. We know that two cars colliding head-on will produce more damage than a car colliding with another car that is standing still. Exactly the same thing happens when a proton collides with another proton that is stationary.

To obtain higher useful energies, it was suggested that the target itself be made to move. In fact, if the two colliding particles were moving in opposite directions, all the energy available would go into the collision. Thus two 20-GeV proton beams colliding head-on produce a useful energy of 40 GeV. A stationary target proton accelerator, on the other hand, would require an energy of 1,000 GeV to make the same amount of energy available.

STORAGE RING ACCELERATORS

Storage ring accelerators use two separate beams traveling in opposite directions around a circular track. The beams are made to collide head-on. The one drawback of colliding beams, however, is that they contain far fewer particles than

even a small solid target. The number of particles that actually collide is therefore much smaller than when a beam hits a stationary target. In the language of the accelerator designer, the "luminosity" of the machine is very low. The function of a storage ring is to give particles more than one chance to collide with each other.

One of the most spectacular examples of the use of storage rings has been the recent development of colliding beams of electrons and positrons. The positron is the antiparticle of the electron, and an example of antimatter. The subject of antimatter will be taken up more fully in a later chapter. It is sufficient to know here that when an electron and a positron collide, they "annihilate" each other to form energy. The final state of the annihilation process has given rise to the discovery of many unexpected new particles.

The technical problems of harnessing beams of positrons are formidable. The positrons are usually produced by allowing a high-energy electron beam to strike a metal target such as tungsten. The positrons formed by the complex reactions inside the target are then separated from the electrons by means of a magnetic-lens system. Both beams are then accelerated to high speeds and made to collide.

Even with the intense beams of electrons and positrons produced in a modern accelerator, the probability of a positron actually colliding with an electron when the two beams are directed at each other is very low. To increase the chance of the particles hitting each other, they are stored in circular rings, called storage rings. Here the beams are made to circulate in closed orbits and allowed to collide over and over again in certain regions where the orbits intersect.

At Stanford University the two-mile (3-km) long linear accelerator runs under Interstate Highway 280 south of San Francisco. Electrons are injected into the machine at the top, accelerated to high energy, and then deflected to several experimental areas at center and bottom.

Many accelerators contain two separate storage rings, one for each beam. There are usually one or two regions where the beams cross each other so that collisions can take place. Often, as in the case of electron-positron beams, known in shorthand as an $e^+ - e^-$ beam, they are made to circulate in opposite directions in the same ring.

SPEAR

One of the largest of the $e^+ - e^-$ storage rings is at the Stanford Linear Accelerator Center and is called the SPEAR (Stanford Positron Electron Asymmetric Ring). The ring, which is underground to guard against radiation, has a diameter about as big as a football field. Sitting on top of the ring are several buildings that contain batteries of lights, cameras, magnets, detectors, and the mammoth hydrogen bubble chambers and spark chambers that actually take photographs of the results of the collisions.

The particles are injected into the ring after being first accelerated through the two-mile (3 km) long linear accelerator. The accelerator can produce particles with an energy of 4 GeV. The total energy available is therefore 8 GeV. It has been estimated that a linear accelerator with a stationary target would have to be approximately six thousand miles (9,660 km) long to produce the same available energy.

Stanford is presently the home of another $e^+ - e^-$ collider called PEP, with a maximum beam energy of 20 GeV. It is planning yet a larger machine to be called the SLC (Stanford linear collider). It is scheduled to be completed by 1986 and should be able to boost the available energy up to 100 GeV.

Not to be outdone, European laboratories are planning even larger colliders, and a host of their own acronyms. A new storage ring called the LEP (large electron positron) is being built at CERN and is scheduled to be completed by 1988. It will be sixteen miles (26 km) in circumference and the energy attainable is expected to be as great as 130 GeV.

Germany can boast of an important 30-GeV collider called PETRA, at the Deutsches Electronen Synchrotron

In this artist's conception, beams of electrons and
positrons from the linear accelerator are deflected into
the storage ring SPEAR and collide. Actually, the beams
continue to circulate in the ring, producing collisions
at both the near and far sides for hours at a time.

The circular shape of the world's highest energy-producing machine, TEVATRON, can be seen in this aerial photograph of Fermilab, near Chicago.

(DESY) near Hamburg. The Germans are planning a new machine, called HERA, to be built by 1990, that will collide 800-GeV protons with 30-GeV electrons.

ANTIPROTON COLLIDERS

To produce some of the strange particles we shall be meeting later, even more energy is required. To supply this energy, colliding beams using another exotic form of antimatter, called an antiproton, are used. When a proton and an antiproton collide, they also annihilate each other, but the possible energy released can be a hundred times as great.

At CERN in Geneva, a proton-antiproton (p-$\bar{\text{p}}$) collider—the bar over the second $\bar{\text{p}}$ denotes an antiproton—has been functioning successfully together with the SPS (Super Proton Synchrotron). Energies of about 80 GeV have resulted in the major discovery of the W particle, a particle whose significance will become apparent later.

The Fermilab, near Chicago, boasts the highest energy-producing machine in the world at the present time. Its TEVATRON can produce protons whose energy is 1 TeV, one trillion electron volts, hence its name. By using superconducting magnets, Chicago plans to build storage rings where protons and antiprotons can collide and produce a colossal center-of-mass energy of 2 TeV.

FUTURE ACCELERATORS

No one can really anticipate the physics and technology of tomorrow. Japan, China, and the USSR are planning gigantic projects whose names would fill this page with a maze of acronyms.

The only factor that is predictable is that the cost of these accelerators will climb astronomically. To go beyond TeV energies would strain the economy of most countries. To cope with this problem, an International Committee on Future Accelerators (ICFA) has been formed in Europe to consider joint proposals and contributions toward the construction of very large accelerators.

In the United States a group called the High Energy Physics Advisory Panel (HEPAP) has the mission of deciding how best to spend federal money for accelerator construction. One of their recommendations has been the superconducting supercollider (SSC). Nicknamed "the desertron," its projected cost is more than a billion dollars, and its size might reach a circumference of one hundred miles (161 km). The plan, which would take more than ten years to complete, has yet to find its way through Congress. Many scientists feel that although it might funnel money from other important projects in physics, it would be a dramatic step toward restoring American leadeship in the field of high-energy physics. The range of possible new discoveries it might make can only be guessed at.

CHAPTER 4
STRANGE FORMS OF MATTER

As physicists penetrated deeper into the nucleus, they began to discover strange forms of matter. Entirely new and intriguing particles were brought to light and became the objects of intensive study. Earliest among them were *mesons, positrons,* and *muons.* Later these were followed by a whole menagerie of other particles.

MESONS

The origin of the strong force, the force that binds neutrons and protons together, had been a puzzle almost from the moment the nucleus was discovered. Very little was known about it. By the middle of the 1930s, however, experiments began to indicate that this nuclear force had a range of only 10^{-13} cm, a distance that is approximately the size of the proton itself. This meant that the neutron and proton had to come very close to one another before they "felt" the attractive nuclear force.

This extremely short range led Hideki Yukawa, the brilliant Japanese theoretical physicist, to propose that the strong interaction results from the exchange of a virtual particle with a very large mass. From the uncertainty relation, Yukawa estimated that his new particle, which had never been observed, must have a mass in the neighborhood of 100 MeV. Physicists routinely express mass in terms of its energy equivalent. Thus an electron is said to have a mass of 0.5 MeV, and a proton a mass of 940 MeV (MeV is the familiar million-electron-volt unit of energy used in our discussion of accelerators in chapter 3).

He called his virtual particle a *meson* ("the intermediate one"), because its mass was between that of an electron and a nucleon. The idea seemed so appealing that the search for the missing meson was immediately taken up by laboratories throughout the world.

Finally, in 1947, after more than fifteen years of frustrating work, Yukawa's particle was discovered. Tracks observed in a photographic emulsion exposed to radiation at high altitudes gave evidence of a particle that had the right mass, a mass close to the one predicted by Yukawa. It was named the primary meson or π (pi) meson (π for *p*rimary). Today it is usually referred to as a *pion,* a contraction of *pi meson.* There was little doubt that the pion, which proved to have a mass of 140 MeV, had many of the properties of the virtual particle associated with the nuclear force. Yukawa's theory had been triumphantly verified.

With the development of particle accelerators, pions can now be routinely produced in the laboratory. Three different kinds of π meson have been identified. A positively charged pion π^+, a negatively charged pion π^-, and an electrically neutral pion π^0. As physicists learned new facts about the strong interaction, however, it soon became apparent that the nuclear force could not be completely explained in terms of pions alone. The search for other particles continued, stimulated by the expanding field of quantum theory.

POSITRONS

One of the most dramatic consequences of this search was the discovery of a new form of matter, called *antimatter.* This extraordinary material exists for a short period of time only, and then vanishes in a cloud of energy. Its behavior seems to be more appropriate to science fiction than to reality.

The existence of an antiparticle equivalent of the electron was first postulated in 1928 by the English physicist, P. A. M. Dirac. Dirac was trying to develop a quantum-mechanical theory of the electron that would satisfy Einstein's special theory of relativity. He found that his solution predicted the existence of a positively charged electron which he called a *positron.*

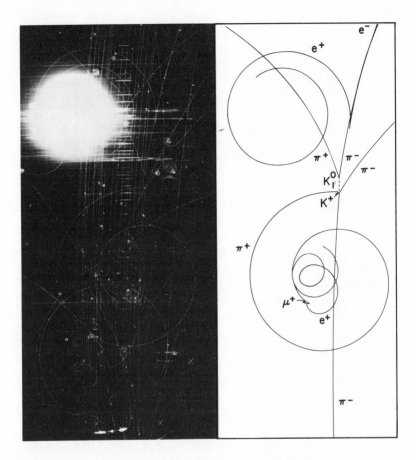

This bubble chamber photograph show a negatively
charged pion (π^-) interacting with a proton to
produce a positive K meson (K^+), a neutral K_1 meson
(K_1^0), shown by the dotted line on the map, a negative
pion (π^-), and a neutron, whose path is not shown.
The K^+ quickly decays into a positive pion (π^+)
and a neutral pion (π^0), whose path is not shown.
The π^+ decays into a positive muon (μ^+), which
decays into a positive electron (e^+). The π^0 decays
into a pair of gamma rays (not shown), one of which
converts into the electron (e^-) positron (e^+) pair.
The K_1^0 decays into a π^+ and a π^-.

At about the same time, Carl D. Anderson of the California Institute of Technology was independently studying the properties of cosmic rays, the radiation falling onto the earth from outer space. He obtained a photographic picture of a track that experimentally established the existence of the positron.

The electron and the positron are antiparticles of each other. The positron resembles the electron in almost all respects. It has the same mass, and exactly the same amount of charge except that the charge is of opposite sign. But it differs in a startling way. When a positron collides with an electron, the two particles destroy, or "annihilate," each other. Both particles disappear and energy is released in the form of photons of electromagnetic energy.

Equally startling was the discovery of the reverse of this process. Under certain conditions photons of electromagnetic energy can interact with atoms to transform themselves into electrons and positrons. Here were dramatic examples of Einstein's theory of the equivalence of mass and energy. The positron was a significant example of a completely new type of particle, one that could be created and destroyed. Physicists were at a loss to explain its role in the atom. How did it fit in with the other elementary particles?

Positrons are not the only antiparticles. In the family of pions, the π^- particle is the antiparticle of the π^+, while the π^0 is its own antiparticle. Recent work has uncovered a host of others. In fact, every particle so far discovered has an antiparticle, a kind of mirror image of the "real" particle. The collision of a particle and its antiparticle always results in annihilation of both particles and the release of energy.

During the past few years physicists have managed to actually create antimatter. An antihydrogen atom, for example, consisting of an antiproton and an antielectron has been made in several laboratories. Unfortunately, the lifetime of antimatter is very short, since it immediately annihilates itself on contact with ordinary matter.

We have already seen, in our discussion of accelerators, that the annihilation energy released in the collision between very energetic electrons and positrons has led to the discovery of many new particles.

MUONS

The cosmic ray studies of Carl Anderson led to the discovery of yet another meson, the μ meson. Found during the search for Yukawa's exchange particle, the μ meson (pronounced mu meson), or muon, resembles an electron in almost every respect. It is some 210 times more massive, however.

The existence of the pion had been expected, but why is there a muon? Why is it so much more massive than an electron? As Isidor Rabi, the Nobel Prize–winning American physicist put it, "The muon—who ordered that?"

It soon became clear that muons were being produced by the decay of Yukawa's pions. Like most of the newly found particles, pions are unstable. That is, after a very brief existence they spontaneously decay into muons and neutrinos. The transformation of a pion into a muon is shown below in equation form, with the neutrino represented by the symbol ν.

$$\pi^- \longrightarrow \mu^- + \nu$$

More surprises were in store for physicists. As they carefully examined the decay of pions, they discovered that the neutrino created along with the muon, now called the muon-neutrino, was a different particle from the neutrino associated with the creation of an electron in beta decay. The two kinds of neutrino share many properties, such as the lack of charge or mass, but when muon-neutrinos interact with matter, different reactions occur.

Muons are themselves unstable. We shall see that almost every elementary particle is unstable. The negatively charged muon lives for a short period of time, about one-millionth of a second, and then disintegrates into an electron and two neutrinos.

QUANTUM NUMBERS

As particles began to proliferate, new ways to characterize them were needed. Describing them solely in terms of their mass and charge proved to be inadequate. Sets of so-called *quantum numbers*, representing different aspects of a particle's behavior, were developed and used. They identified the particles almost like telephone numbers.

When a property of the atom is given a quantum number, it is said to be "quantized." The term implies that the range of its possible values is limited in some way. Only certain numbers are possible. Quantized phenomena can occur in the most ordinary way. When you throw a pair of dice, for example, the numbers that turn up are limited. You can throw a 7, or an 11, but never a 7½. The result of the throw must obviously always be a whole number. The set of possibilities then—integers running from 2 to 12—is an example of a set of outcomes that mathematicians describe as being quantized.

One of the most striking characteristics of the quantum-mechanical description of the subatomic world is that so many of its properties are quantized. For example, electric charge is quantized. It seems to come only in chunks of the basic unit of charge possessed by the electron. The charges carried by all other charged particles are observed to be multiples of this elementary number. Thus the charge of a positive pion is $+1e$ (e stands for the charge of the electron), that of a positron, $+1e$, and that of a negative muon, $-1e$.

The orbital motion of an electron about the nucleus of an atom is also quantized. The electron can move only in certain permitted orbits. Each of the allowed orbits is defined and determined by an orbital quantum number.

SPIN QUANTUM NUMBERS

An electron in an atom behaves somewhat like the earth in its daily rotation about the sun. It spins on its own axis as it orbits about the nucleus. Because the electron is spinning, it has rotational inertia. Physicists call it *angular momentum.* The angular momentum describes, among other things, how fast the electron is spinning.

One of the great discoveries of quantum physics is that in the world of the atom, angular momentum is quantized. There are only a certain number of rates of angular spin possible. Almost all the particles that have been discovered are found to be spinning. Their spins are also quantized. The rate of spin is designated by a quantum number called the spin quantum number. It describes how fast the particle is rotating in terms of some basic rate of spin. The spin of the electron, for example, is one-half this basic rate, and so the electron is said to have a spin quantum number of ½. Protons, neutrons, and muons also have spin ½. Surprisingly, photons also have spin. These particles, associated with light, and other forms of electromagnetic energy, have a spin of 1. Pions, on the other hand, are found to be spin-0 particles, indicating they are one of the few particles in nature that are not rotating.

FERMIONS AND BOSONS

The spin quantum numbers of every particle are always observed to be either integral, such as 0, 1, or 2, or half-integral, such as ½ or ³⁄₂. Surprisingly, particles with half-integral spins do behave quite differently from particles with integral spins when they are grouped together in a system such as a nucleus or an atom. Because of this, particles are classified according to whether their spin is integral or half-integral. Particles with half-integral spins are called *fermions,* in honor of Enrico Fermi, who first described the behavior of this class of particles. The corresponding description of particles with intergral spins was the work of the Indian physicist Satyendra Nath Bose. These particles were named *bosons.* According to this classification scheme, pions and photons are bosons, while electrons are fermions.

PAULI EXCLUSION PRINCIPLE

An important property of fermions, first recognized by Wolfgang Pauli in 1925, is known as the *exclusion principle.* It states that when fermions are grouped together in some system, as in an atom or nucleus, no two of them can have the same set of quantum numbers. Almost like saying that two objects cannot be in the same place at the same time, the exclusion principle states that no two fermions can be in the same quantum "place," or state, at the same time.

This rule is one of the most important in understanding atomic structure. It explains, for example, why the electrons in large atoms do not all crowd together in the lowest energy state, the one closest to the nucleus. Electrons are spin-½ particles, and are therefore fermions subject to the exclusion principle. The electrons must distribute themselves about the nucleus in such a way that no two of them are in the same quantum state. The electrons are, in a sense, forced to occupy the higher energy levels.

Whether a particle is a fermion or a boson will prove to have other important consequences, as we shall see in a later chapter.

CHAPTER 5
THE
PARTICLE
ZOO

A list of the known particles compiled in the late 1940s would basically have included all the particles that have been so far described. Then, in a relatively few years, the field of particle physics exploded. New particles began to be discovered with startling rapidity and the list of elementary particles grew to over thirty within the next eight years. This period of great productivity was due primarily to the experimental use of a new generation of particle accelerators of much higher energy. After a brief pause that led to the development of new techniques of detection and still higher-energy machines, the count jumped again, to well over the one hundred particles we know of today.

THE NEW PARTICLE
EXPLOSION

One of the first of the new particles to be discovered turned up in reactions initiated by cosmic rays. The collision between protons and nuclei produced an unknown particle that appeared to be heavier than a proton. The reaction was observed in a bubble chamber, a device used to record the passage of high-energy particles in the laboratory. As a particle passes through such a bubble chamber, it leaves visible tracks that can be photographed and then analyzed.

Physicists computed the lifetime of the new particle from the length of the track it made in the bubble chamber, and found that it lived an unusually long time before disintegrating. On the basis of the appearance of these tracks, which reminded many experimenters of the letter V, the new "strange" particle was called by the Greek letter lambda (Λ).

More particles were soon seen. The development of accelerators opened the floodgates to a host of other strange particles. Most of them were given Greek names. The new particles were of two basic types, mesons such as the K mesons and rho (ρ) mesons, whose mass was between that of an electron and a nucleon, and heavy particles, such as the lambda (Λ) particles, the sigma (Σ) particles, the xi (Ξ) particles, and the delta (Δ) particles, whose mass was greater than that of a proton.

The table at the end of this chapter presents a partial list of some of these particles. The array of Greek symbols is a bit uncomfortable to read, but it is obviously a large list of supposedly "fundamental" particles. You might notice that the particles are arranged in clusters or families. The three sigma (Σ) particles, for example, form a group of approximately the same mass, but with different charges. The two xi (Ξ) particles form a similar group, as do the neutron and proton.

The masses of these particles seem to have no logical connection, however, and there seems to be no reason for so many particles to exist. Physicists despaired of ever making sense of what came to be called "the particle zoo."

A new way of classifying the particles helped scientists bring some order to what seemed chaotic. All the known particles were divided into groups based on whether or not they were sensitive to the strong interaction. Those particles that interact by means of the strong force are called *hadrons* (from the Greek *hadros,* meaning "strong"). Those particles that are not susceptible to the strong force, on the other hand, are called *leptons* (from the Greek *leptos,* meaning "small"). Most of the particles are hadrons. A few, like the photon, fall into neither category, and are unique in the subatomic world.

LEPTONS

Leptons are the most mysterious of all particles. They appear to have no internal structure, and apparently have no size.

The leptons all have spin ½ and are therefore fermions. Until quite recently, there were just four known leptons: the electron, the muon, the electron-neutrino, and the muon-neutrino. Each of the four leptons has an antilepton.

Since they are not subject to the strong interaction, the force that binds nucleons together, the leptons have great power to penetrate matter. A muon, for example, even one that carries an electric charge, can penetrate many meters of lead before it is stopped by the electromagnetic interaction. As for the neutrino, we have seen that it can pass through thousands of miles of earth and not interact with anything.

A search for additional members of the lepton family was undertaken in 1974 by a group of physicists at the Stanford Linear Accelerator Center (SLAC), using the SPEAR electron-positron storage rings. The energy produced by colliding electrons and positrons created large numbers of new particles. It was hoped that a new lepton might be one of the possible particles formed in this way.

After much arduous labor a new lepton was indeed identified, and called a tau (τ) particle. Along with it came yet another neutrino, the tau-neutrino. Like the muon, the τ particle was unstable and decayed within 10^{-13} seconds. The mass of the τ particle, however, was a surprise. With its measured mass of approximately 1,800 MeV, it was close to four thousand times the mass of an electron, and approximately twice the mass of a proton. In spite of its mass there was no doubt that it was a lepton. It was a new variety—a heavy lepton.

HADRONS

The hadrons are complex particles. Unlike the leptons, they appear to have an internal structure made up of still more fundamental particles, the quarks. Most of the hadrons are unstable, and disintegrate to form other particles.

It is customary to subdivide the hadrons into two smaller groups of particles named *baryons* and mesons. The division is made on the basis of the products of their decay. Those particles that eventually form a proton are called baryons, and the rest are called mesons.

The baryons (from the Greek *baryos,* meaning "heavy") are generally heavier than the mesons, and include the familiar proton and neutron. The mesons include such particles as the pion. Because the baryons are fermions (their spin quantum number is measured in half-integral values, such as ½ or ³⁄₂), they obey the Pauli exclusion principle. Mesons, on the other hand, have integral spin values such as zero or one. This has important consequences for the behavior of the two kinds of hadrons.

As a result of discoveries made over the past two decades, the baryons and the mesons have grown into very large families of particles. There are, in all, more than one hundred known hadrons, most of them massive and unstable.

We shall see that it was this great proliferation of hadrons that led to the formulation of the quark model. Baryons will be shown to be composed of three quarks, while mesons are made up of a quark and an antiquark.

CONSERVATION OF BARYONS

As physicists looked at the formidable list of hadrons, they began to notice certain interesting patterns. When the baryons were created in large accelerators, for example, they never appeared singly, but always in pairs, as baryons and antibaryons. Furthermore, when the baryons decayed, they always produced another baryon. The baryons never seemed simply to disappear. It was as if the baryons had some special property they were passing on to each other.

This behavior is an example of what physicists call a conservation law. A quantity is said to be conserved if it doesn't change during some physical process. Electric charge, for example, is said to be conserved because the total charge present in any system undergoing a reaction never changes. When it appears to be destroyed, as when a negatively charged electron undergoes annihilation with its antiparticle, the positively charged positron, and both disappear, the net change of electric charge in the event is nevertheless $(+1) +$

(−1) or zero. Baryons were also recognized as obeying the same kind of conservation law. Baryons can be neither created nor destroyed except in pairs of real baryons and their corresponding antibaryons.

BARYON NUMBER

The resemblance of the behavior of baryons to electric charge prompted physicists to introduce a simple, convenient system of bookkeeping. Baryons were assigned a new quantum number, called the baryon number, of +1, and antibaryons were assigned the quantum number −1. When a baryon and its antibaryon disappear, the total change in baryon number is simply (+1) + (−1) or zero. Similarly, when a baryon and its antiparticle are created, the change in baryon number is also zero. It is convenient to rephrase the conservation of baryons into a form easier to use by saying that the baryon number is conserved—that is, it never changes in any observed interaction. The other members of the hadron family, the mesons, were not affected by a similar conservation law, and were assigned the baryon number of zero.

ISOTOPIC SPIN

A further attempt to simplify the almost overwhelming array of particles that seemed to exist in nature was made by Werner Heisenberg. Heisenberg reasoned that neutrons and protons, which resemble each other in so many respects (except for electric charge) might appear different only because of the electric field produced by the proton. Somehow the electric field destroyed the sameness of the two particles. If the electric charge could magically be "turned off," perhaps the two would be identical. Using this analogy, Heisenberg proposed that the proton and neutron were "up" and "down" states of the same particle. It was as though an imaginary arrow were attached to a particle. When the arrow pointed up, it was a proton. When the arrow pointed down, it was a neutron.

Heisenberg then invented a new quantum number, which he called the isotopic quantum number, or *isospin* for short. Unlike the spin of an electron, however, which was a measure of angular momentum, isospin was a purely abstract concept that had nothing to do with "real" spin. It was a purely imaginary spin assigned to particles within families that resembled each other in almost every way except in electric charge.

The neutron and proton form a family of two nucleons. By analogy with the electron, they were assigned isospin quantum numbers of $+\frac{1}{2}$ for the neutron and $-\frac{1}{2}$ for the proton. Isospin numbers were then assigned to other families on the basis of the number of particles within each group. The family of pions, for example, with three similar members, π^+, π^-, and π^0, was assigned an isospin number of 1. The three pions were given isospin values of $I = +1, 0,$ or -1, depending on the kind of charge they carried.

Artificial as they may seem at this point, these imaginary isospin rotations proved to be of great value. It was soon established that the isospin number, like the baryon number, obeyed a conservation law. The discovery that isospin is conserved in the strong interactions was, as we shall see in the next chapter, an important step in understanding what reactions could or could not occur in nature.

STRANGENESS

Most of the hadrons are unstable. After a certain period of time, which can be as small as 10^{-23} seconds, they disintegrate into less massive particles such as protons, mesons, and neutrinos. Certain hadrons, however, like the Σ and the Ξ particles, were observed to live for a very long time before decaying. The amount of time they required to decay, about 10^{-10} seconds, was puzzling. A tenth of a billionth of a second might not seem very long, but compared with the lifetime of 10^{-23} seconds, which is characteristic of many other hadrons, it seemed an eternity. To put the difference of time in a slightly different way, if the lifetime of a typical hadron were one second, the slower decaying Σ particle would live one million years. Because of this unusual behavior, the long-lived hadrons were referred to as *strange particles*.

PROPERTIES OF SOME HADRONS AND LEPTONS

Name	Symbol	Charge	Mass (MeV)	Spin	Baryon Number	Strange- ness
Baryons						
Proton	p	+1	938.3	½	1	0
Neutron	n	0	939.6	½	1	0
Lambda	Λ^0	0	1,116	½	1	−1
Sigma	Σ^+	+1	1,189	½	1	−1
	Σ^0	0	1,193	½	1	−1
	Σ^-	−1	1,197	½	1	−1
Xi	Ξ^0	0	1,315	½	1	−2
	Ξ^-	−1	1,321	½	1	−2
Omega	Ω^-	−1	1,673	3⁄2	1	−3
Leptons						
Electron	e^-	−1	0.511	½	0	0
Muon	μ^-	−1	105.7	½	0	0
Electron- neutrino	ν_e	0	0	½	0	0
Muon- neutrino	ν_μ	0	0	½	0	0
Mesons						
Pion	π^+	+1	139.6	0	0	0
	π^0	0	135	0	0	0
	π^-	−1	139.6	0	0	0
Kaon	K^+	+1	493.7	0	0	+1
	K^0	0	497.7	0	0	+1

As the large accelerators began to produce more strange particles, physicists soon noticed that these always occurred in pairs. This immediately suggested a conservation law similar to the law of conservation of baryons. We start with no strange particles and end up with two of them. If one of the particles had a positive strangeness quantum number, and the other a negative strangeness quantum number, the sum would be zero. We start with zero strangeness, and end with zero strangeness. Strangeness is conserved in strong interactions.

By an elaborate system of bookkeeping based on the average charge of families of particles related to each other by isospin, a strangeness quantum number is assigned to every particle. The nucleons have a strangeness of zero, as does the family of three pions. The lambda particle, on the other hand, has a strangeness of -1, while the K meson has a strangeness of $+1$.

We shall see later that the long life of strange particles is the result of weak interactions rather than of the strong interaction that produces them in nucleon collisions. Weak interactions, you will remember, are involved in radioactive decays as well. Unlike some of the other properties of hadrons, strangeness is not conserved in weak interactions.

A table listing some of the leptons and hadrons, along with their properties, is shown on page 45.

CHAPTER 6
QUARKS

As the machines for looking into the world of the atom became larger and more energetic, they reached the point where they could probe deeply into the heart of a nucleon itself. Scientists realized that the neutron and proton were not simple, fundamental particles after all. They too were complex structures made up of still smaller bits of matter. The possibility that basic structures simpler even than a nucleon existed was an exciting and revolutionary idea. It raised the hope, always central to modern physics, that the huge number of observed baryons and mesons were only different combinations of a few really fundamental particles.

THE EIGHTFOLD WAY

In the early 1960s a new pattern emerged among the strange particles that eventually led to a more profound understanding of the structure of matter. Previous studies of the hadrons had shown that almost all of them could be grouped into small family units. The neutron and proton, for example, belong to a family with two members, and the pions to a family with three members. Among the known particles the size of the family ranges from one to four members. Physicists call such family groupings *charge multiplets*. Within a multiplet, like the triplet of pions, the members all have approximately the same properties except for charge.

A new form of organization was suggested in 1961 by Yuval Ne'eman, an Israeli army colonel turned physicist, and

Murray Gell-Mann of the California Institute of Technology. Working independently, they both discovered a hidden symmetry among the particles that led them to suggest grouping them into even larger families, or *supermultiplets*.

The new system was called the *eightfold way* because it involved eight quantum numbers, and recalled, at least to its creators, a somewhat farfetched reference to a saying attributed to the Buddha. "Now this, O monks, is noble truth that leads to the cessation of pain: this is the noble Eightfold Way: namely right views, right intention, right speech, right action, right living, right effort, right mindfulness, right concentration."

The mathematical basis of the eightfold way is a branch of mathematics called group theory. Group theory is a very powerful mathematical technique for dealing with such symmetry operations as reflections and rotations. If you take a book on a table, and rotate it 360 degrees through a full circle, the book will be exactly back in its original position. This rotation is an example of a symmetry operation. Symmetry operations of this kind had already played a large role in pointing out similarities among various hadrons. We have seen, for example, that the neutron and proton can be thought of as being related through the rotation of a make-believe arrow in the fictitious world of isospin space.

The eightfold way is generated by a comparison between the particle families and the behavior of a special kind of group dealing with symmetries, the SU(3), invented by the nineteenth-century Norwegian mathematician Sophus Lie. The theory revealed that the hadrons should be able to form extended families, or supermultiplets, of one, three, eight, or ten members. The groupings were assigned according to the quantum properties of the particles.

THE OMEGA-MINUS PARTICLE

Most of the known particles (there are more than a hundred of them) were placed in these superfamilies and seemed to fit the theoretical system very well. Gell-Mann noticed, however, that one of these large families seemed to be incomplete. Instead of finding ten members, he could find only nine. Gell-Mann then made a very dramatic prediction which captured the attention of the scientific world. On the basis of the eight-fold way, he described what the missing particle should look like. He specified the mass, charge, and quantum numbers of the missing particle, and even named it the *omega-minus* (Ω^-) *particle*. Successful predictions of this kind are one of the hallmarks of a valid physical theory.

The family Gell-Mann was looking at consisted of a group of delta particles (Δ^-, Δ^0, Δ^+, Δ^{++}), sigma particles (Σ^-, Σ^0, Σ^+), and xi particles (Ξ^-, Ξ^0). When these particles, arranged according to their mass, are placed on a graph that plots isospin against strangeness, the broad outlines of a pyramid appear (see figure 2).

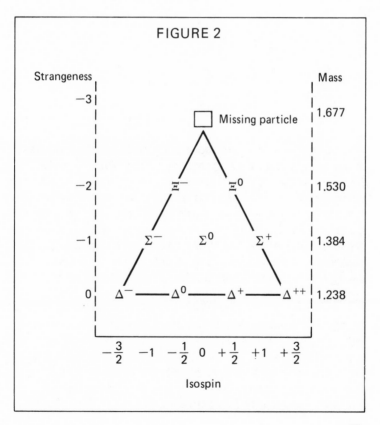

FIGURE 2

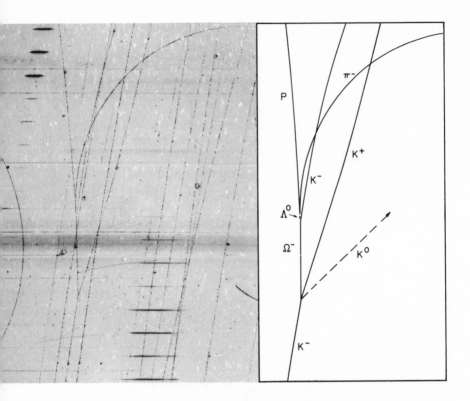

This bubble chamber photograph is the third observation of the production of a negatively charged omega meson (Ω⁻). The map to the right shows the proper assignments of a particle to each track. The paths of neutral particles, which produce no bubbles in the liquid hydrogen and therefore leave no tracks, are shown by the dashed lines. The presence and properties of the neutral particles are established by analysis of the tracks of their charged decay products or the application of the laws of conservation of mass and energy, or a combination of both. The incoming K^- meson collides with an unseen, stationery proton with the resultant production of a neutral K meson (K^0), a positive K meson (K^+), and the negative omega meson (Ω⁻). The Ω⁻ decays, after a lifetime of about one ten-billionth of a second, into a neutral lambda baryon (Λ⁰) and a negative K meson (K^-). The Λ⁰ then decays into a proton (p) and a negative pion (π^-).

The top of the pyramid, shown by the empty square, appears to be missing. One can predict that it should have a strangeness of −3, a negative charge, and a mass of 1.677 GeV.

The search for the missing omega-minus particle was taken up in 1963 by the 33-billion-electron-volt accelerator at Brookhaven National Laboratory. Using the lab's brand-new 80-inch (203 cm) bubble chamber as a target, some fifty thousand photographs of events were obtained after several months of operating the machine twenty-four hours a day. Finally, tracks were identified that confirmed the actual production of the omega-minus particle.

Whatever skepticism scientists originally had about the eightfold way soon disappeared. The successful prediction of the omega-minus particle was simply too impressive. As Sheldon Glashow, the 1979 winner of the Nobel Prize in physics, said, "The omega-minus particle made converts of us all."

QUARKS

The regularity of the eightfold way was puzzling. What was the meaning of the symmetrical families that formed in groups of eight and ten? Why, if the eightfold way predicted supermultiplets of three, were none observed among the hadrons?

It was the missing three elements of the group that led Murray Gell-Mann and George Zweig, also at the California Institute of Technology, to suggest independently in 1964 that the eightfold way could be explained if all the hadrons were made up of a family of three elementary constituents. Gell-Mann playfully named these new particles *quarks*. His inspiration came from a passage in James Joyce's *Finnegan's Wake*: "Three quarks for Muster Mark! Sure he hasn't got much of a bark. . . ."

Gell-Mann suggested that there were three kinds of quarks. To use his language, the quarks came in three distinct "flavors": the up, or u-flavored, quark; the down, or d-flavored, quark; and the strange, or s-flavored, quark. The names are quite arbitrary, and a bit whimsical, and there are many physicists who find these names unfortunate.

One of the most distinctive features of the quark model is that quarks are required to have charges that are fractions of the charge on the electron. This seems to contradict one of the most commonly accepted observations that electric charge always comes in integral multiples of the electron's charge. The charge of every known hadron can be accounted for, however, by assigning the up quark a charge of +⅔, the down quark a charge of −⅓, and the strange quark a charge of −⅓.

Three corresponding antiquarks were postulated: the antiup, ū, the antidown, đ, and the antistrange, s̄. The antiquarks all have charges that are opposite their quark counterparts, and are denoted by writing the quark symbol with a bar over it.

QUARK COMPOSITION

The quark composition of every hadron could now be accounted for by very simple rules. Baryons are formed by combining three quarks, and mesons are formed by combining two. In the case of the mesons, the two always consist of a quark and an antiquark.

To make sure that such conservation laws as the conservation of baryon number and conservation of strangeness are not violated, several other quantum numbers are assigned in addition to charge. Each quark is assigned a baryon number of +⅓, and a spin of ½. Strangeness is handled by giving the up and down quarks a strangeness number of zero, and the strange quark a strangeness of −1.

THE THREE FUNDAMENTAL QUARKS

Name	Symbol	Charge	Spin	Baryon number	Strangeness
Up	u	+⅔	½	⅓	0
Down	d	−⅓	½	⅓	0
Strange	s	−⅓	½	⅓	−1

Each antiquark has exactly the same quantum numbers, but with its numerical sign reversed. The antiup quark, for example, has a charge of $-\frac{2}{3}$, a baryon number of $-\frac{1}{3}$, and a spin of $-\frac{1}{2}$.

To see how the quark model works, let's look at a proton. It is made up of two u-quarks and a down quark (uud). To determine the properties of the proton, we simply add up the assigned numbers.

$$
\begin{array}{rccccccc}
 & u & & u & & d & & \\
\text{Proton charge:} & (+\tfrac{2}{3}) & + & (+\tfrac{2}{3}) & + & (-\tfrac{1}{3}) & = & +1 \\
\text{Proton baryon number:} & (+\tfrac{1}{3}) & + & (+\tfrac{1}{3}) & + & (+\tfrac{1}{3}) & = & +1 \\
\text{Proton strangeness:} & (0) & + & (0) & + & (0) & = & 0
\end{array}
$$

In the case of a typical meson such as the positive pion, it is composed of an up quark and an antidown quark (u$\bar{\text{d}}$). Summing, we get:

$$
\begin{array}{rccccc}
 & u & & d & & \\
\pi^+ \text{ charge:} & (+\tfrac{2}{3}) & + & (+\tfrac{1}{3}) & = & 1 \\
\pi^+ \text{ baryon number:} & (+1) & + & (-1) & = & 0 \\
\pi^+ \text{ strangeness:} & (0) & + & (0) & = & 0
\end{array}
$$

The strange quark is needed to construct the strange particles. The neutral lambda particle, for example, is composed of an up quark, a down quark, and a strange quark (uds).

$$
\begin{array}{rccccccc}
 & u & & d & & s & & \\
\Lambda^0 \text{ charge:} & (+\tfrac{2}{3}) & + & (-\tfrac{1}{3}) & + & (-\tfrac{1}{3}) & = & 0 \\
\Lambda^0 \text{ baryon number:} & (+\tfrac{1}{3}) & + & (+\tfrac{1}{3}) & + & (+\tfrac{1}{3}) & = & 1 \\
\Lambda^0 \text{ strangeness:} & (0) & + & (0) & + & (-1) & = & -1
\end{array}
$$

Simple diagrams of these hadrons are shown in figure 3. The antiquarks are represented by hatched lines.

A table of some baryons and mesons giving their quark structure is given on page 54.

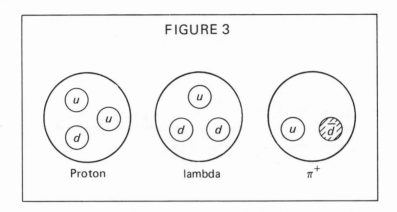

FIGURE 3

Proton | lambda | π^+

QUARK STRUCTURE OF SOME BARYONS AND MESONS

Name	Symbol	Quark Structure
Baryons		
Proton	p	uud
Neutron	n	udd
Lambda	Λ^0	uds
Sigma	Σ^+	uus
	Σ^0	uds
	Σ^-	dds
Xi	Ξ^0	uss
	Ξ^-	dss
Omega	Ω^-	sss
Mesons		
Pion	π^+	$\bar{d}u$
	π^0	$\bar{u}u$
	π^-	$\bar{u}d$
Kaon	K^+	$\bar{u}s$
	K^0	$\bar{d}s$

Every strange particle contains at least one strange or one antistrange quark. The omega-minus particle seems to be the champion of strange particles and contains as many as three s-quarks. The conservation of strangeness we observed in the last chapter can now be interpreted as implying that any s-quarks contained by the strange particle must be passed along intact to the decay products. If the possible decay products are not composed of s-quarks, the transition essentially cannot occur. We shall see in a later chapter, however, that as a result of weak interactions, an s-quark can be changed into a u-quark or a d-quark, so that the strange particle can decay, but only through weak interactions. This helps to explain why the decay of some strange particles is inhibited and takes an unusually long time.

QUARK SPINS

Can the quark theory explain why mesons only have integral spins such as 0 or 1, or why baryons only have half-integral spins such as ½ or 3⁄2? Yes, since we have seen that every quark has a spin of ½.

To understand how, consider the spin of a meson. Mesons are made up of a quark and an antiquark. The spins associated with each quark can either point in the same direction or in opposite directions. In the first case the spins add to give a total of 1. In the second case the spins cancel each other, like two bar magnets canceling each other's magnetic field, and give a total spin of 0.

Baryons, on the other hand, contain three quarks. If the possible spin orientations for baryons are added together in the same manner, some spin is always left over because we are dealing with an odd number of quarks. The result is always a half-integral spin, either ½ or 3⁄2.

These spins can be visualized in the diagram (see figure 4):

The theory of quarks was an impressive account of the structure of particles. Every known hadron could be explained as a combination of quarks. What is more, every allowed combination of quarks corresponds to a known hadron.

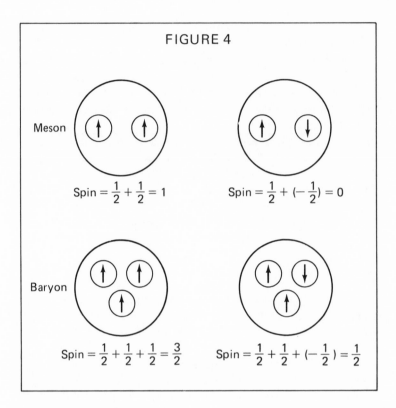

FIGURE 4

Meson

$$\text{Spin} = \frac{1}{2} + \frac{1}{2} = 1$$

$$\text{Spin} = \frac{1}{2} + (-\frac{1}{2}) = 0$$

Baryon

$$\text{Spin} = \frac{1}{2} + \frac{1}{2} + \frac{1}{2} = \frac{3}{2}$$

$$\text{Spin} = \frac{1}{2} + \frac{1}{2} + (-\frac{1}{2}) = \frac{1}{2}$$

LOOKING INSIDE A PROTON

In spite of its remarkable successes, the quark theory met with a great deal of hostility in the physics community. The idea of a particle with a fractional charge was hard to swallow. After all, no such particle had ever been seen. Was it a real particle or just a mathematical fiction? Particle physicists have hunted for quarks for years, and none have been found. What is it, if quarks really exist, that prohibits them from appearing by themselves?

The first direct evidence for their existence came in a series of deep-scattering experiments performed at the Stanford Linear Accelerator Center (SLAC). Electrons were accelerated to energies of up to 20 billion electron volts in a two-mile (3 km) long accelerator, and made to collide with protons. At these energies, the electron could penetrate deeply into the proton.

The electrons were observed to scatter through wide angles. The results were similar to the original experiment by Rutherford that first demonstrated the nuclear atom. An analysis of the scattering pattern of the electrons indicated that the proton contained three "hard" constituents that were electrically charged.

The internal structure of the proton revealed by these experiments corresponds very closely to the quark model. A closer analysis indicated, however, that the proton contained other constituents as well. We shall see in the next chapter that these additional particles are called *gluons,* the exchange particles that bind quarks together.

CHAPTER 7
A NEW THEORY
OF MATTER
—COLOR FORCE

*T*he success of the original quark theory lasted only a short while. Hard questions began to be asked about disturbing violations of some universally accepted principles of quantum mechanics. The quarks have a spin of ½, and therefore are fermions. We have seen that fermions must obey the Pauli exclusion principle, the quantum-mechanical way of saying that no two fermions can be in the same quantum place at the same time. But many of the quark systems proposed for hadrons appeared to violate this very fundamental principle.

The omega-minus particle, for example, is made up of three strange quarks, all identical. Since each of the three quarks has a spin that must be either "up" or "down," at least two of them must have exactly the same spin. These two quarks will have all their quantum characteristics the same—the same flavor, the same charge, and the same spin. They are therefore in the same quantum state, in direct violation of the exclusion principle.

THE COLOR HYPOTHESIS

The impasse was finally resolved in 1964 by Oscar W. Greenberg of the University of Maryland. He solved the problem by simply inventing a new quantum number. This new quantum number could be used to differentiate between similar quarks. The quantum number he manufactured had three possible values. By assigning a different value of this quantum number to each of three similar quarks, he could immediately separate them into different quantum states. The omega-minus particle with its three strange quarks could "legitimately" exist without violating the exclusion principle.

This new quantum number has come to be known as *color.* Each of its three possible values was identified by a different color. Although physicists avoid any association of real colors with these quantum numbers, the colors red, green, and blue seemed as good a choice as any, and were generally adopted. A strange quark, then, is really three different particles, a red s-quark, a green s-quark, and a blue s-quark. It is important to remember that none of these color labels has anything to do with real color—quarks are not painted particles.

To be consistent with this completely imaginary color designation, the antiquarks were assigned anticolors that were complementary to the primary colors. Thus the antiquark of a red quark was labeled cyan, the antiquark of a green quark was magenta, and the antiquark of the blue quark was yellow. Since it has proved difficult to remember all these colors, physicists usually refer to the antiquarks as antired, antigreen, or antiblue.

The color hypothesis, while solving the problem of identical quarks, presented some difficulties of its own. No one had ever detected color in a particle. Either it was invisible or, as one physicist put it, nature is "color-blind." Since hadrons appear to be colorless, the logical assumption was made that the quark colors somehow cancel each other out. Protons, neutrons, and the other baryons are made up of three quarks. Each of them must therefore have a different color. These abstract quantum "colors" combine, like the real primary colors, to leave no net color. The color force, then, leads to the binding together of three quarks only if each of them has a different color. (Figure 5 demonstrates the color hypothesis. Each of the strange quarks that make up an omega-minus particle has a different color and therefore can exist in the same space without violating the exclusion principle.) Any other combination never occurs and must therefore be disruptive.

Mesons, you will remember, are made of only a quark and an antiquark. If the meson is to be colorless with only two colors to combine, the two colors must consist of a color and

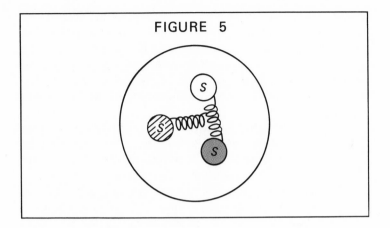

FIGURE 5

its anticolor, say blue and yellow (or antiblue). Here again, the color force will bind together two quarks only if they are paired as a quark and an antiquark.

COLOR FORCE

The color quantum number was first used to explain how quarks of the same flavor could exist in a hadron without violating the Pauli exclusion principle. With time, however, the concept of color, or color charge, as it is now sometimes called, took on more meaning than had first been anticipated. It soon became apparent that color charge served, in much the same way as electric charge serves in electromagnetic interactions, to explain the forces and interactions between quarks.

The theory of color force is called *quantum chromodynamics* (*chromo* means "color"). Just as the force between electric charges is transmitted by a virtual photon, the force between quarks is transmitted by a virtual particle called a *gluon*. The gluon "glues" the quarks together. Like the photon, it is a massless particle with spin 1. Unlike the photon, however, which is a neutral particle, the gluons themselves are also colored. To complicate matters a bit more, there are eight different gluons made up of combinations of color and anticolor.

Since a gluon carries color, it can change the color of the quarks it interacts with. For example, the absorption of a gluon might change a red quark into a blue quark. The green quark emitting a gluon could be changed into a red quark. The exchange of gluons does not, however, change the flavor of the quark. A d-quark remains a d-quark, and a u-quark remains a u-quark.

An interesting consequence of a gluon having a color charge is that gluons can interact with each other through the color force. Two gluons should be able to attract each other and form a "color particle" held together by the exchange of other gluons. These strange objects, called glueballs, have never been observed but are under intensive investigation.

The color force is responsible not only for the force between quarks but also for the nuclear force. The more familiar strong interaction between hadrons, such as the force binding a neutron to a proton in a nucleus, is really the result of the interactions of the two sets of three quarks that make up these particles.

QUARK CONFINEMENT

If every hadron is made up of quarks, why has a quark never been seen? With enough energy, it should be possible to free a quark from its confinement within a particle. This has never happened. In order to explain this, we have to assume that the color force acts in exactly the opposite fashion from the other interactions. We all know, for example, that when the distance between two magnets is increased, the force between them decreases. When the distance between two quarks is increased, though, the force of attraction appears to increase.

This strange behavior can possibly explain why individual quarks have never been observed. Hadrons have been examined in accelerators using projectiles with energies large enough to penetrate them to their very core. The results of these so-called "deep-scattering" experiments seem to show that quarks are moving about rather freely inside a hadron. The quarks behave as though there was a very feeble bond between them. A fast-moving projectile should be able to dislodge them very easily. Yet this never happens.

Although the quark is not constrained within the inner recesses of a hadron, as the quark begins to separate itself from the other quarks, the force between them grows rapidly.

The three quarks within a proton, for example, seem to be tied to each other by loose, elastic "strings" of gluons. They are free to move about, and feel no forces, as long as they remain within the limits of the strings. As soon as they try to exceed these bounds, however, strong forces are produced that keep them from flying apart. This color force is the strongest known force encountered in nature. It would take almost an infinite amount of energy to separate quarks.

A CHARMED QUARK

In 1974 a new particle was discovered independently by two competing teams of experimental physicists. One group, working at Brookhaven National Laboratory, chose to call it the J particle. The other group, working at the Stanford Linear Accelerator Center (SLAC), decided to name their particle the psi (Ψ) particle. In an astonishing display of an idea whose time had come, the announcements of the discovery were made within hours of each other. Both teams were given credit for the discovery. The group leaders of the two teams, Samuel C. C. Ting of MIT and Burton Richter of SLAC shared the Nobel Prize in physics in 1976. Today, since neither team was willing to relinquish its claim to name the particle, it is called the J/Ψ particle.

The J/Ψ particle was startling because its existence seemed to threaten the validity of the quark theory. The group at Brookhaven called its discovery "the November uprising." The problem with its existence was that there was simply no room for it in the quark scheme of things. The J/Ψ was definitely a meson, since it had a spin of 1, yet it could not be formed by any allowed combination of quarks. There was no way of juggling the quarks about to form the particle.

The new particle was surprisingly massive, with a mass three times that of a proton. Like the other heavy hadrons, it was unstable, but its lifetime was about one thousand times longer than that of most hadrons. It reminded physicists of another particle, the phi (ϕ) meson, that had been discovered some years earlier. The phi meson had a lifetime of the same order of magnitude as the J/Ψ particle. The phi meson, however, was known to be made of a strange quark and an antistrange quark. Its long life was explained as being due to the relatively long time required for the quark and its antiquark to annihilate each other during its decay.

Rather than abandon the quark theory, physicists resorted to a way out of the impasse, a way they had found to be very fruitful in the past. They invented a new quark. It was assumed that the J/Ψ particle was made up of this new quark "flavor," one that had previously been overlooked. This fourth quark was called a *charmed quark* and was designated by the letter c. Its counterpart in the antiworld was the anticharmed quark, $\bar{c}$. Using the phi meson with its comparable lifetime as an example, the J/Ψ particle was assumed to be composed of a charmed quark and an anticharmed quark ($c\bar{c}$).

The validity of this new quark would depend, of course, on whether other particles could be found that also contained the charmed quark. It was to be expected that the new quark would combine with the three original quarks to form great numbers of new hadrons. The search for particles that contain charm proved difficult. The first to turn up was called a D^0 meson with a quark composition of antiup and charm ($\bar{u}c$). Another meson, called an F meson, with a quark composition of antistrange and charm ($\bar{s}c$), was subsequently found, as was a charmed baryon, the charmed lambda particle (Λ_c) with a (udc) quark composition. Since 1980 many other charmed particles have been found. The evidence for the charmed quark was overwhelming.

A QUARK NAMED "BEAUTY"

The discovery of the charmed quark was exciting but a bit disturbing to many scientists. The number of "fundamental" particles seemed to be growing again in a fashion reminiscent of the flood of hadrons that appeared during the 1960s.

This feeling of unease was certainly not helped by the discovery of another massive particle that pointed the way to yet a fifth quark. In 1978 a group of investigators using the proton synchrotron at the Fermi National Accelerator Laboratory (Fermilab) discovered a new particle with a mass of 9.4 GeV (billion electron volts). This electrically neutral meson was the heaviest particle ever observed. Its mass proved to be as great as ten times the mass of a proton.

The new particle was called the upsilon (Υ) particle. It was unstable, but it had an unusually long lifetime. Its decay seemed to be inhibited. When it finally did decay it did not disintegrate into hadrons that were combinations of the four known quarks. The new particle behaved in much the same way as the J/Ψ particle.

By the same sort of reasoning that had been successful with the J/Ψ particle, it was assumed that the upsilon particle was composed of a new quark "flavor" bound to its antiquark. This fifth variety of quark was called *beauty* or *b-quark* (the name "bottom" is also used by some physicists). Careful studies have shown the charge of the b-quark is $-\frac{1}{3}$.

A QUARK NAMED "TRUTH"

In order to construct a parallel to the six known leptons, theorists had predicted that if a fifth quark were discovered, there would also be a sixth. The name chosen for this symmetrical counterpart to beauty was *truth* (the name "top" is preferred by the same group that uses "bottom" for the fifth quark). The t-quark has not yet been observed experimentally, but few physicists doubt its existence.

The catalog of quarks is growing. With six basic quarks and three possible colors, there are now eighteen varieties of quark. There is no doubt that the quark model has been highly successful. Several hundred hadrons are now known, and they all can be classified and described in terms of quarks.

Is the number of quarks limited, or will other quarks be found as accelerators become larger and more energetic? Is it possible that a quark itself has an internal structure? There are no answers to these questions now. But as the energy available in our large atom smashers begins to approximate the energy during the first few moments of creation as postulated in the "big bang" theory, physicists feel they are coming closer to a truly "fundamental" particle.

CHAPTER 8
GRAND UNIFICATION THEORY

*U*ntil quite recently, the four forces that govern the behavior of every particle of matter—the gravitational, electromagnetic, strong, and weak—appeared quite different from one another. They differed in their strength, their range, and in their exchange particle. Many physicists now believe, however, that they all derive from a single fundamental force.

Recent studies seem to indicate that the similarities among the four forces are hidden by the rather special circumstances under which they are being observed. The forces appear to have separate properties only at the relatively low energies of the world we live in. At high energies, comparable to the energy available during the first few seconds following the process that created the universe, the so-called "big bang," it is believed that a unification of all these forces occurs. All the forces become identical.

The attempt to find a unified theory explaining the different forces has been a long-standing goal of physics. Historically the concept of unification began in the late nineteenth century with the work of the celebrated Scottish physicist, James Clerk Maxwell. He was the first to recognize that electricity and magnetism were really two manifestations of the same basic force, electromagnetism. But how did the other three forces fit in? Albert Einstein spent the last years of his life in a fruitless attempt to go beyond the work of Maxwell.

The path toward unification came from a rather unexpected source—the weak interaction. The weak interaction, you will recall, is the mechanism by means of which certain radioactive reactions occur. In an important step toward understanding weak interactions, three distinguished physicists, Sheldon Glashow, Steven Weinberg, and Abdus Salam, found a way to unify the weak interaction with the electromagnetic interaction. They called the combined, unified force the *electroweak force.*

The electroweak theory, for which they were awarded the Nobel Prize in 1979, identifies the carriers of the weak force as massive virtual particles called "vector bosons." These exchange particles, you will remember, resemble a ball being tossed back and forth. They induce a reaction in the emitters and receivers of the particle.

There are three different kinds of exchange particles involved in the weak force. Two of them are electrically charged and one is electrically neutral. When the charged particles are exchanged, the reaction is said to be a "charged current" reaction. When the neutral boson is exchanged, the reaction is called a "neutral current" reaction. Taking their name from the first letter of the word *weak,* the charged particles were called W^+ and W^-, while the neutral boson particle was called a Z particle.

Weak decays generally proceed in two steps. The first step always involves the emission of a virtual vector boson. The decay of a neutron into a proton and electron, for example, is a typical reaction that is mediated by the weak force.

$$n \rightarrow p + e^- + \bar{\nu}$$

It is described by assuming that the neutron first decays into a proton and emits a virtual W^- particle. The W particle then changes into an electron and a neutrino. (See figure 6.)

The search for the particles was taken up at CERN, the European Center for Nuclear Research. This consortium of thirteen nations worked for five years before they finally confirmed the existence of the W and Z particles. Over a million events were recorded and subjected to laborious, painstaking analyses. It was a great triumph for the electroweak theory. The W and the Z particles had a measured mass of 84 GeV, in excellent agreement with predicted values. It is this large mass that explains why the weak interaction proceeds so slowly.

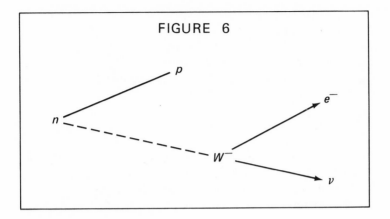

FIGURE 6

SYMMETRY BREAKING

The mathematical theory that led to the electroweak force successfully demonstrated that the electromagnetic and weak forces were different aspects of the same force, mediated by the exchange of the same family of four particles. They predicted that at high temperatures, roughly 100 trillion degrees centigrade, the particles should all be massless and have a spin of 1. At lower temperatures, however, temperatures comparable to those observed in the real world, some of the exchange particles are transformed. A process called *symmetry breaking* transforms three of the massless particles into the W and Z particles, with a mass predicted to be approximately 100 GeV. The fourth particle, identified with the photon, remains massless. In other words, the two forces have a double identity at low energies only. At higher energies they should merge into one combined electroweak force.

The electroweak theory has correctly predicted the masses of the W and Z particles, and they have been experimentally observed. Another prediction of the electroweak theory that is particularly striking is that the weak force should increase in strength, while the electromagnetic force should decrease, at higher energies. Studies have shown that the approximate energy at which the forces would unify and lose their separate identities is about 100 GeV, an amount of energy too large for us to produce in any machine at this time. It is believed, however, that such quantities of energy were available during the "big bang" that created our universe. There is a good chance that in an earlier, "hotter" universe only a single force existed. This force then separated into different forms as the universe cooled.

THE DECAY OF
THE PROTON

The success of the electroweak theory has led scientists to hope that there might also be a way of unifying the strong force with the weak and electromagnetic forces.

To unite the strong force with the electroweak force, physicists have developed a theory that requires an exchange particle with an incredible mass of 10^{15} GeV. These particles—twelve of them are predicted—are named X bosons. They have the ability to turn quarks into leptons and leptons into quarks. A red X boson, for example, with a charge of 4/3 can combine with an anti-red down quark to produce a positron. Although there is no accelerator with enough energy to produce a particle with this much mass, it should be detectable by the decay of the proton.

We have seen that a proton is made up of three quarks. Through the exchange of an X particle it should be possible to transform one of the quarks into an electron or positron. Such a reaction would result in the decay of the proton. The idea of an unstable proton is rather startling. Not only does it mean that under certain conditions baryons are not conserved, but after all, every atom of matter contains protons. A radioactive proton would imply that everything in the universe will eventually disappear into leptons and photons of energy.

THE SALT MINE
DETECTOR

The hunt for a decaying proton is nevertheless being undertaken in a salt mine two thousand feet (610 m) below Cleveland, Ohio. Using a detector as big as a six-story building consisting of eight thousand tons of water, a team of physicists from the University of California at Irvine, University of

Michigan, and Brookhaven National Laboratory hope to be the first to see a proton decay. The experiment is being conducted in a salt mine so that other forms of radiation, always present at sea level, will not interfere with this elusive event.

Similar experiments are being done under Mount Blanc in the Alps, and also in India. The results to date have been negative. The expected decay of a proton into a positron and pion has not been seen. It certainly is an unlikely event, since the mass of the postulated X particle, 10^{15} GeV, is almost unimaginable. The lifetime of a proton has been shown to be greater than 10^{31} years, billions and billions of times greater than the estimated age of the universe itself. If the protons are eventually found to be unstable, it will be a triumph for theoretical physics, but bad news for the universe. Don't be alarmed, however. It would take a near eternity for all matter to turn into energy.

GRAND UNIFICATION THEORY

One of the major goals of modern physics is to create a model of the universe that will see all physical forces as part of one all-encompassing interaction.

The electroweak force has provided the beginning of such a model. There is some hope that the search for the X boson in proton decay will be successful in relating the color force to the electroweak force.

The merger of the strong and electroweak forces is called the *grand unification theory* (GUT.) Like the Weinberg-Salam theory, it postulates that at high enough temperatures, the forces are identical. The temperatures at which GUT becomes effective, however, are in the neighborhood of an almost inconceivable 10^{27} degrees centigrade. The new unified force is thought of as being transmitted by a family of twenty-four massless exchange particles. At the lower temperatures of our observable universe, the process called symmetry breaking again separates the basic force into two seemingly different forces, the strong and the electroweak. The exchange particles now are converted into gluons, vector bosons, and X particles.

The grand unification theory has yet to be experimentally verified. The discovery of an unstable proton would be very dramatic evidence for its validity, and has become a major goal of experimental physics.

GRAVITONS

The gravitational interaction, however, is still the most difficult of the four fundamental forces to integrate into a unified theory. The gravitational interaction has always been difficult to deal with. It is so feeble that if an atom depended on gravitational forces instead of electromagnetic forces to hold it together, the atom would have to be bigger than the observable universe. The problem of relating gravity to the other forces is extremely complex.

During the past decade a new theory of gravity, called *supergravity,* has been developed. It incorporates many of the ideas of quantum mechanics into a description of the gravitational interaction. (See figure 7. The interaction between particles can be thought of as being transmitted by a virtual particle.) As with the other forces, the interaction is thought of as being transmitted by a virtual particle called a *graviton.* To be consistent with the other exchange particles, the graviton is also a vector boson, but with the unusual spin of 2. Because of its long range, it must be a massless particle.

SUPERSYMMETRY

The theory of supergravity is really part of a more general theory called *supersymmetry.* The mathematical way of describing the theory is very complicated because it is expressed in terms of symmetry operations.

The concept of symmetry has always been very important in the description of the physical world. The fact that every particle has an antiparticle was first predicted, for example, on the basis of symmetry arguments. Supersymmetry establishes an analogous pairing between the fermions and bosons. It proposes that for every fermion there exists a corresponding boson, and for every boson there

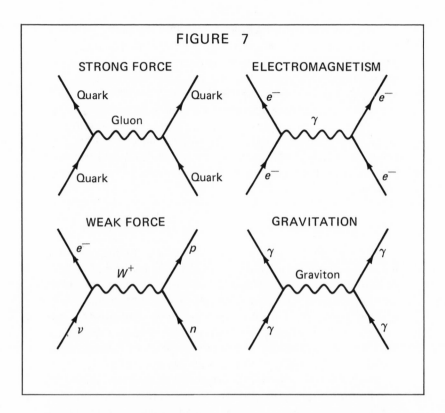

FIGURE 7

STRONG FORCE

Quark   Quark

Gluon

Quark   Quark

ELECTROMAGNETISM

e^- e^-

γ

e^- e^-

WEAK FORCE

e^- p

W^+

ν n

GRAVITATION

γ γ

Graviton

γ γ

exists a corresponding fermion. The proposed names for the supersymmetrical counterparts of the particles are rather amusing, and continue the tradition of whimsy established with the quark. The symmetry partners of such bosons as the photon, gluon, and graviton, are the *photino,* the *gluino,* and the *gravitino.* Fermions like the quarks and leptons have supersymmetric boson partners called *squarks* and *sleptons.* None of these new particles have been observed.

The simplest supergravity theory describes a world consisting of gravitons and gravitinos. At low temperatures, the force of gravity comes about through the exchange of gravitons. At high temperatures, pairs of gravitinos are exchanged resulting in a force comparable in strength to the other forces.

Another theory, known as an extended supergravity theory—there are actually eight sets of these theories—has extended the number of symmetrical particles to include all the exchange particles of all the forces. These particles can be thought of as being different states of one basic "superparticle." A symmetry operation such as reflection or rotation can transform the superparticle into a quark, an electron, a gluon, or a graviton. There are still mathematical difficulties associated with these theories, but it is hoped that they will play an important role in explaining the unity of the forces of nature.

TECHNICOLOR

As though nature were constantly putting obstacles in the way of any attempt to simplify the universe around us, a possible new fundamental force called the *technicolor* force has recently been postulated. The new force was proposed to explain the baffling problem of how the unified electroweak force actually separates into two distinct forces, the electromagnetic and the weak. In the language of a physicist, what "breaks the symmetry" of the electroweak force?

In the technicolor theory, proposed by Stephen Weinberg and Leonard Susskind, the problem is solved by introducing yet other hypothetical particles, called *Higgs mesons, techniquarks,* and *technipions.* At the moment, the only accelerator capable of testing this theory by supplying enough energy to possibly find these particles is being built at CERN in Switzerland. It is scheduled to be completed in 1987, and a search for these "techniparticles" has already been made part of the approved experimental program.

THE FUTURE

It is obvious that much has been learned about the structure of our universe during the past fifty years. The progress made with the introduction and development of quantum electrodynamics and quantum chromodynamics has been spectacular. A grand unification theory is within the realm of the possible for the first time.

Can gravity be included in a superunification theory? Was there one fundamental force at the moment of creation? We are within reach of answering these questions. A history of past unification theories can be traced in the diagram below (see figure 8) to show how a superunification theory could be attained.

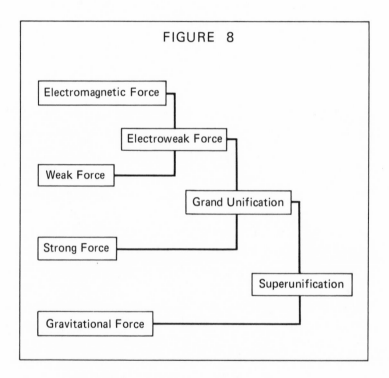

FIGURE 8

Larger and larger accelerators are scheduled to be built in this country and abroad. They should be able to test and refine some of the revolutionary ideas presented. Some of these ideas should not only give us knowlege of the ultimate constituents of matter, but also allow us to understand the very origins of our universe.

GLOSSARY

Angular momentum—A quantitative measure of the amount of rotation or spin of elementary particles.

Antimatter—Matter that consists of antiparticles, such as antiprotons, positrons, and antineutrons. Antihydrogen, for example, the antimatter analog of ordinary hydrogen, consists of an antiproton and a positron. When antimatter comes in contact with ordinary matter, both are annihilated, and their mass converted into energy.

Baryons—One of the subgroups of particles with half-integral spin that participates in the strong interaction. The group includes the neutron and proton. Baryons are among the most massive of the elementary particles.

Bosons—A name given to particles such as the photon (spin = 1) and the π meson (spin = 0) that have zero or integral spin.

Color—A label given to a special attribute of a quark. It comes in three varieties, red, green, and blue, and has nothing to do with "real" colors that we can see. The color of quarks determines the magnitude of the strong interaction between them.

Electroweak force—The basic force predicted by the electroweak theory. The unification of the weak interaction and the electromagnetic interaction predicts that the weak force and the electric force are simply two different manifestations of a single, more basic force, the electroweak force.

Exclusion principle—A general statement about the behavior of elementary particles. First discovered by Wolfgang Pauli, it states that no two fermions can be in the same quantum state at the same time.

Fermions—A name given to such particles as the electron (spin = 1/2) and the proton (spin = 1/2), which have half-integral spins. These particle all obey the Pauli Exclusion Principle.

Gluons—The uncharged virtual particles that mediate the interaction between quarks.

Grand unification theory—The theory that states that the known forces of nature—gravity, electromagnetic, strong, and weak—are all different manifestations of a single basic force. Its most startling prediction is that the proton is unstable.

Graviton—The particle that mediates the force of gravity. This particle has not been observed, but it should be massless and have a spin of 2.

Hadrons—The class of particles that participates in the strong, or nuclear, interaction. They are composite objects, being made up of quarks. The hadrons are subdivided into two further groups of particles, baryons and mesons; the baryons have half-integral spin (1/2, 3/2, . . .), and the mesons have integral spin (0, 1, 2, . . .).

Intermediate bosons—The supposed carriers of the weak nuclear force. They have finally been observed at CERN and named W and Z particles.

Isospin—An abstract concept, developed by analogy with the electron spin, that considers the neutron and the proton as two states of one particle, the nucleon. To describe the two states, the proton and the neutron are considered as the up and the down isospin state of the nucleon.

Leptons—The class of particles that does not participate in the strong interaction. They interact primarily via the electromagnetic force. The leptons include the electron, the muon, and the neutrinos. They all have spin 1/2, and appear to have no internal structure.

Mesons—The family of particles whose masses are between those of the leptons and the baryons. The mesons have spin of 0 or 1.

Muon—A negatively charged particle that is unstable and is included in the family of mesons. It resembles the electron in most respects except that it has a mass 207 times heavier.

Neutrino—"Little neutral one" in Italian. It is a massless, electrically neutral particle, first observed along with the electron, in the emission of certain radioactive elements. It is now known that there are three different kinds of neutrino: the electron-neutrino, the muon-neutrino, and the tau-neutrino.

Nucleon—Either a neutron or a proton. Because of their similarity, these particles are classified together as nucleons.

Photon—The particle, or "bundle" of energy, first postulated by Albert Einstein, to explain the way light and other forms of electromagnetic energy are emitted and absorbed by matter.

Pion—An unstable meson that is considered to be the mediator or carrier of the strong nuclear force. Denoted by the Greek letter π (pi), the name comes from *pi*-mes*on*.

Positron—The positively charged antiparticle of the electron. When a positron collides with an electron, they annihilate each other and both are converted into energy.

Quantum—First used by Max Planck in 1900 to explain the radiation given off by an ideal blackbody. Planck suggested that atoms could only absorb or reradiate energy as a small package he called a quantum of energy.

Quantum chromodynamics—The name given to the theory that describes the interaction between quarks and gluons.

Strange particles—A group of unstable particles with unusually long lifetimes. It includes such particles as the Λ^0 and the K^0.

Uncertainty principle—The theory first enunciated by Werner Heisenberg in 1927 that states that there is a limit on the accuracy with which we can do experiments. The simultaneous measurements of position and momentum of a particle, for example, cannot be made arbitrarily precise. The more accurately we know the position of the particle, the greater the uncertainty in its momentum.

Virtual particle—The name given to the unobserved particles that are thought of as the intermediary by means of which forces are transmitted between particles.

Weak force—One of the four basic forces that exist in nature. Much weaker than the other forces that influence nuclear particles, it is responsible for the relatively slow process known as nuclear beta decay, as well as all reactions involving neutrinos.

INDEX